CU00767373

*A Translated Man*

*Also by Robert Sheppard*

**Poetry**
*Returns*
*Daylight Robbery*
*The Flashlight Sonata*
*Transit Depots/Empty Diaries*
            (with John Seed [text] and Patricia Farrell [images])
*Empty Diaries*
*The Lores*
*The Anti-Orpheus: a notebook*
*Tin Pan Arcadia*
*Hymns to the God in which My Typewriter Believes*
*Complete Twentieth Century Blues*
*Warrant Error*
*Berlin Bursts*
*The Given*

**Fiction**
*The Only Life*

**Edited**
*Floating Capital: New Poets from London* (with Adrian Clarke)
*News for the Ear: A Homage to Roy Fisher* (with Peter Robinson)
*The Salt Companion to Lee Harwood*
*The Door at Taldir: Selected Poems of Paul Evans*

**Criticism**
*Far Language: Poetics and Linguistically Innovative Poetry 1978–1997*
*The Poetry of Saying: British Poetry and Its Discontents 1950–2000*
*Iain Sinclair*
*When Bad Times Made for Good Poetry*

Robert Sheppard

*A*
*Translated*
*Man*

Shearsman Books

First published in the United Kingdom in 2013 by
Shearsman Books
50 Westons Hill Drive
Emersons Green
BRISTOL
BS16 7DF

Shearsman Books Ltd Registered Office
30–31 St. James Place, Mangotsfield, Bristol BS16 9JB
(this address not for correspondence)


www.shearsman.com


ISBN 978-1-84861-284-6

Copyright © Robert Sheppard, 2013.
The right of Robert Sheppard to be identified as the author
of this work has been asserted by him in accordance with the
Copyrights, Designs and Patents Act of 1988.
All rights reserved.

# Contents

# THE SECRET PLAYER:
## RENÉ VAN VALCKENBORCH AND
## HIS DOUBLE OEUVRE

This book is the result of an incredible story.

In the spring of 2004 two youthful translators met at a conference I organised, Translational Conflictions, at Leuven, not in itself an auspicious thing to happen. When it is revealed that one of the translator's specialisms was to translate from the Dutch language group and that the other was an expert in Francophone literatures, it might have been expected that, other than the theory of translation, there would be nothing to hold them together. They were both participating on a panel on contemporary literary translation and a remarkable thing happened, as I knew it would, having read their abstracts in advance and paired them. Martin Krol, who is from South Africa, and is an authority on Flemish poetry, and Annemie Dupuis from Quebec, who is a specialist in Walloon literature, discovered not only that they were speaking about translating the poetic work of my homeland, that most linguistically and bitterly divided of modern European nations, Belgium, but that they were speaking about the work of the same poet, René Van Valckenborch. What they discovered—and what had apparently been kept hidden from the literary schools of my country, separated as they are not just by language but by culture and regional autonomy—was that Van Valckenborch was writing in both languages and was publishing two distinct bodies of work, one initially in Canada and the other partly in South Africa, as well as in Europe: in Rouen, Amsterdam, and in Belgium itself.

Both translators imagined that they were the first to apply themselves to Van Valckenborch. There was surprise and laughter for, after Krol had delivered his paper 'Aprosody as Cognitive Mapping', Dupuis declared herself unwilling to read her contribution, 'The Return of the Mind to Things', and extemporised a series of fascinating challenges to herself and Krol (and me) about this extraordinary circumstance. After initial mutual suspicion, and diplomatic manoeuvres on my part during a coffee break, they agreed to work together to solve the mystery: how could, and why would, one writer produce two discrete oeuvres? Their initial answers required them to engage in further translations, email exchanges across continents, and occasional meetings over the next few months. This is not the place to enquire further into their liaison, but after Martin took up a post in Brussels, interpreting for the EU, Annemie moved there too, to work as freelance translator. They lived together, and married in 2006 (but separated in 2010, it seems, about the same time this story unravels).

One of the delights—but occasionally one of the disappointments—of translating contemporary works is meeting their authors. As soon as the couple settled in Brussels, they insist, they set about searching for Van Valckenborch. It had not been unusual for his publishers to only deal with him by email and post – but cybernetic and street addresses failed to yield a reply, and ringing on suggested doors did not materialise the man. Stalking the noisy dope-hazed bars of Vlaamsesteenweg—a 'clue' from one of the poems, Krol explained—asking crag-faced bikers after a man of whom they had not even the vaguest description proved fruitless, as did hushed enquiries at the Poëziecentrum, located at 'a forlorn corner' of a square in Ghent (another clue). The man had vanished, or as in one of Magritte's paintings that seems to encapsulate Belgian surreality, his figure offers his back to us, as does his double in the mirror beyond him. For not only did the man disappear, his work stopped appearing. The bookshop at Ghent was to furnish the last substantial chunk of his work in Flemish, *A Hundred and Eight Odes*, and a final Walloon fascicle, *cow*—a direct reference to Magritte's 'période vache'—was reportedly picked up by Dupuis in a sale in a sunny bilingual shop in Antoine Dansaertstraat in Brussels, not far from their apartment. A website, containing a selection of work by European poets (clearly all made up) no sooner clicked onto by me than deleted, left a single link to an enigmatic Twitter feed that claimed to be Van Valckenborch's daily mini-proclamations to the world.

The idea that this extraordinary body of work was a hoax naturally arose. Perhaps it was a counter-hoax, some commentators suggested, to the one perpetrated by RTBF when it broadcast spoof reports of Flanders' declaration of independence from Belgium in December 2006. (Incidentally, this occurred four days before our translators were married and the processions of monarchists through Brussels interrupted their festivities, to which I had been invited!) The existence of a genuinely bilingual contemporary poet in Belgium seems too good, or bad, depending on one's perspective, to be true. However, someone had to compose these verses and although suspicion has fallen upon the two translators—critics speculate that the confrontation in Leuven was staged, the 'original' poems written backwards from their double 'translations', charges I refute as Byzantine absurdity—the fact remains that the poems exist, and demand to be read. (Of course, suspicion has fallen upon myself also, particularly since Dupuis and Krol seem not to answer calls or reply to letters or emails, indeed seem to have left Brussels, if not Belgium, if not Europe…). I am not denying that the poetry's ontological status is unchanged by questions of what would once have been called 'authenticity', but it remains a truth that these poems face us uncertainly with this lack of facts—again, not unlike Magritte's canvasses, which often offer us monumental but obscured central enigmas. The unease which this situation evokes, cannot be willed away by transferring these texts into Gerald Bruns' convenient category of 'fictional poems'.[1] They demand to be read as poems, as interventions in the world of form, whatever their provenance, which, in my opinion, should have little influence upon the reading process or their reputational reception. In that spirit, I welcome you to a selection of translations into English, edited by myself, arranged here in their double manifestations, each in chronological order. Some of the translations betrayed signs of hasty execution and I have been forced to amend them silently, occasionally without the benefit of an original. I have appended a brief bibliography of these works for the specialist, and the original volumes are cited in the contents page.

Erik Canderlinck
formerly of the Institute of Literary Translation,
Leuven
2013

---

[1] Bruns says, in a suggestive passage: 'To be sure, the difference between a poem in a novel and a poem in an anthology is apt to be empirically indiscernible. To speak strictly, a fictional poem would be a poem held in place less by literary history than by one of the categories that the logical world keeps in supply: conceptual models, possible worlds, speculative systems, hypothetical constructions in all their infinite variation—or maybe just whatever finds itself caught between quotation marks, as (what we call) "reality" often is.' Bruns, Gerald L. *The Material of Poetry*. Athens and London: The University of Georgia Press, 2005: 105-6.

# Select Bibliography

Poetry in Walloon (trans. Annemie Dupuis)
: *thingly* 2001
*masks & other masks* 2002
*violent detachments* 2003
*the twelfth noise in the twelfth row* 2004
*glance poems* 2005
*ovid's twistier & new amores* 2006
*emoticon* 2008
*cow* 2010

Uncollected Prose
: 'An Uncertain but Adequate Hold over the Thing',
*Poeticological Digest* (2003): 4.
'Frozen Cuts of Light: The Scratch Cinema of Paul Coppens',
*Chosement* 1 (2010): 46-9.

Poetry in Flemish (trans. Martin Krol)
: *The Light and Other Poems* 2001
*The Fuck Me Shoes Chronicles* 2002
*Rooms and Revolutions* 2008
*A Hundred and Eight Odes* 2010 (includes *Twitterodes*
(tweets 2008-9 @www.twitter/VanValckenborch.com)
*European Union Of Imaginary Authors: 27 Translations*
(website and electronic media) 2008-10

Uncollected Poem
: 'Untitled', *een klap* 7 (1996): 56.

Uncollected Prose
: 'Aprosody: a poetics manifesto', *een klap* 16 (2004)

# Walloon Poems

*translated by Annemie Dupuis*

# from *thingly*

*At last the fidelity of things opens our eyes*
—Zbigniew Herbert

## 2 *scissors*

closed they've a single
point & purpose perfected
cool blades left sleeping

open a dancer—
limbs of flexing steel leap in
frozen cuts of light

## 5 *orthoceus paperweight*

bloated with
blood or water the
simple life-form

points the wrong way its
supposed head noses
ahead of ghostly segments

it mimes the point
of its containment
a uniform chain that trails

away to its point a trial
impression for a
chinese paper dragon

an imperfection inserted
into limitless grey
a worm reduced

to texture of slate like
a varnished pumice that
can never dissolve it stops

all flights of fancy
holding paper to its
promise to persist

fingers smooth the
split-slate surface
of its base pick it

up a man-made pebble it fits
into the curve the hollow
human palm

## 6 *spectacles from the era of léopold I*

arms unfold but
are spikes now
having lost their ear

pieces they could cost
you an eye putting
them on its

joints still open
a genius for survival
the oblate lenses

fringed with rust
in simple metal
frames

between them a nose rest
curved like the moustaches of
the era

a flicked curl at
the extremity of each
holding the lenses

of 1860 focussed
to the narrow
vision of things

a royal canal
trenched through the marsh
the rising of the bourse

& french words around
things among a
clutter of things

unfrench


17 *machine*

the machine
chomps
unoiled hinges

not taking itself
too seriously the waste
basket recycling bin

never catches its bits
not quite evading
metaphor

machine for manufacturing
pairs of
nothing

        drops
pure meaningless
atoms


## 20 *thing*

there's no such
thing space age
arrowhead stone

age laser it
occupies its vacancy
a blade of sky

advertising its handle
of earth promising
spangly girls on spinning

disks a white wheel
hole in a coin
a smile cut from air

no
thing present but
a pure absence within

which we construct
something for a hero
to cut teeth on paper

look again
yearn to skin a liar
it's buried to the hilt

in the flesh of
shadow it marks

a shallow grave

that fills itself
with song
       thingly

# from *masks*

1
*modern mask ghana*

(reverse view)

hollow of smoothed hackings

born violently from wood
for pure spirit or nothing
(like) a consciousness to quiver

construct the inside
of your new face
a concave mirror

for your voice that coughs
apologies to neophyte
& tourist alike

pick it up place it
before your face &
become

*showman shaman*
*sham & shameless hero*
*shapeshifter shoplifter*

look through it at the woman
pawing her face radiance
of sun disk framed by

slots of air steal her
fumes through the mouth as she
ravishes her mask for beauty

3
*modern mask ghana*

*front view*

   *mounted on a wall*

spout moon mouth of
spirit language gushes
you! look! listen!

(sketches of
face-shapes are hardwired into
our recognition drives)

eyes convex ovals hold
a-human twin slits a hint
of surveillance

from the other side (you've
been there you know there's nothing
no one there but your slightest movement

doubts you) metal cheeks of peppered
hammer blows eyebrows of
bevel pits bolted to skin

in symmetry above/below eyes
all bound by a circular band
earth-red in which wave-forms play

pure energy scored seashore frown
on a sanded forehead (bristles
of sea-beard rhyme beneath)

three tears filed free of
varnish wash pearl
pips from the fruited eyes

but above the top & tailed fish
scaled nose a forehead
of wooden hair strains

a frontal lobe
nudging into the world
an invasive fist of mind

that echoes the mouth
which rather than speaks
sucks

into its black hole
a whirlpool withdrawing
its eternal guttering moan


4
*congo-brazzaville*

enface river with half-
horizon loop-cropped grimace
scarred flesh proud

crested hairdo blunt
eyes concentric rings
around holes filled with hole

isolated in the hollow tree
rustling towards the sacrificial
experiment

nothing missing but chiselled
teeth for only the sorceress in her trance
may bite

9

*navajo*

fingers
        ruffle the
scalp its matted horsehair
soul birth

wrap a hide too
small for saddle into
bare life face

gouge eyeholes
mouth hole but nose
—nostrils—not drilled

paint white zig
zags down one cheek
that breathes under them

as they mould a man
plant a single feather
for affect ready

for the plains alert
to sky's tremulous
messages where

birds peck this wig
for nests beaks poke
eye peeped worm holes

stab eye as mask becomes
body itself in(-)
animate art life god

with no voice or vice
cast-off man staggers
against horizon a sky

trickling sand a landscape
gifting abyss until such
aloneness engenders

heroics enacts wind
revives riverbed
summons cloud mr

rainwater his
dry quill rustling with
distant unfelt breeze

       he falls to earth
       & human sweat
       flushes laughing


15
*gas mask first world war flanders*

strapping your head into
the theriomorphosis of the grub
a rubbery frown folds over yours

gaze of supernal sunken
eyes glazed rings of the
pneuma's vigil over mud

in place of mouth a divine cylinder
a proboscis extrudes
a can of maggots

deep rattling of the sieved voice
through perforations a frigid
filtering of tellurian poisons


17
*mask collection tristan tzara kwélé*

                                slanted slit eyes lift
                                into the skies art &
                                potbellied potlatch

                                        memory
                                all poems are naked
                                masks behind western eyes


18
*naked mask stick beating chorus* guéyomlo *ivory coast*

                        (excerpt)


                        -- _ - ..
                         -- _ - .
                        -- _ - ... .


                        -- _ . _ ----
                         --_-....._
                        -- _ . _ ---


                        -- ___ - ...
                         -- _ ..
                        -- ___ ......

```
··__ˉ··__ˉ····__
··__ˉ··__ˉ····__ˉ
·············· ˉ
```

20
*rubber hood anvers*

voice here teeth
snap air
with dungeon breath

superhero dentificaton misi-
dentification
insect sex pitch

sheen to touch smooth
unhuman
integument tight

inswathed with crow
inumbration of hard embrace
intumescing pod pellicle

& rind
scalp & sable
alp

sutured skull
for needles of light
lips

pursed by
rubber skin into a
rouged pout red

spectacles (hand-
cuffs' trauma) ring dead
eyes flickering flashes lashes

a funnel for fake
ponytail to plume
smooth swart head

pierced moist nostrils
seep the chain
at the throat throttles the last word

free

## the stylisation of objects: homage to jan švankmajer

one button on a thread
threatens banister
shadows tangle

slow feet on stairs
wrinkled windfall stuffs
your listening mouth

plaster blossoms
into cavities with brick
skeletons grilles rust

blooms on locks &
chains pebbles trussed
sound scored by scuffed hand

pendulous nose tap
stiff stop cock
dead bell bent nails worm

under blinking light shunting
hinges past the eye vacant peep
holes solid stones both

thunder doors erupt with-
out welcome on vespertine
passages their walls floors

hold brittle cracks together
shattery slate trembles from
shape textured to dust

                 brick-window
shut
     ear

stones dance grind
mottled rind erosion
is form erasure style

making eyes masking
stonyness the venus
of the backyard kisses

& sucks & fucks & splits
broken open to show the
heart of stone is stone

# from *violent detachments*

## *ap(h)orisms*

> *lest the shadow makes the object of this object disappear*
> —Hélène Prigogine

### *violent detachments 1*

there is passage boundary
there is hero heroine voicing ear
giving body as passage we like

the likeness we like the likeness of things but
even if we saw we would never know them
a wilderness of bewilderment fills with relics

vertiginous knots unravel before us
we write things down with cosmic appetite
things conditioned by their inaccessibility

inexpressibility the poem guffaws
black laughter
expulsive force emotion

eclipsed in motion reason
by rhythm the sketchbook gestates
through erasure the appearance

of the muse
is a media problem the dis-
appearance of echo into her own ear is not

## violent detachments 3

stuttering around things
that now speak for us
implicated in history's dives

we are complicated
complicit even
light flows like blood

while
mirrors lift the sky
to the petrifying gaze

of the poet over
the shivering body
of the poem shrinking before

him (her) *you*
*must change your*
*death* mask

chorus over the mind's
dead slogans while
the heart's work is

of valve & vessel
intelligible resemblances
assemble without measure

the breath of thunder
dark stone turned sound
turns then i turn to stone

scratching the dirt
of the world with a
hand that bears no name

silence out there darkness
in here depth wrapped
round the surface of it all

*brazilian jubilee*

1 *zinnia yellow*

colours as
abstract qualia
a colour chart

a tone row for
symphonic rooms
not yet composed

in houses not yet built
for consciousnesses
not yet formed

> *fool's gold*
> *duckling*
> *oasis*

three antique writers
on the next table
famous for 'exactitude'

triangulate
attention between their
wine glasses focus

upon 'yellowy'
muscudet the menu
discuss verhaeren &

their decrepitude
but miss you (whom they claim)
unfolding your 'restaurant

napkin notepad' & building
the case against them word
by word

*mustard seed*
*sunspot*
*king's gold*

gunshots overdub
a crime scene still
montage sequence of

childhood snapshots &
holiday videos milky
edges sharp edits the

real colour of blood
bleeds
process without end


## 2 thoughts of a chinese poem

frost on the oblique
windscreen of the green
smart car is not ice it's

more like sweat that
peels off in the
steam of sunrise

until it's so unlike
itself that it becomes
the clean air

itself last night
the moon's frozen light was
clear & white as snow

before even
the full moon itself composed
itself above the roofs 'sad

it's sad
that words don't' you said
full-on

no shadow
but the language of
shadows we touch


3 *not yet written*

drenched he could have peeled
the strip of crime scene tape from
the wet pavement picked up history's

scent beating impatience a dog's
tail nose to pane peering into
darkness intent on darkness

it's not over until the flat note goes
until the branch is stripped bare
every pip squeaked in its turn

& then to start again with blue this time
making eyes veins veils walls skies
the twelfth noise in the twelfth row

*background pleasures*

*book one*

new poem naked
clapping hands
waiting for applause?

        in the pré-metro just
        enough of a blonde to
        compact desire 'the

        shape of the poem
        determines our tram
        ride beneath brussels'

        in the café verlaine
        the chinese lanterns wilt
        for another new year

camera's eye stares
but attention
jumps between two

men who squeeze dialogue
from corners of their
mouths agree

footnotes are
better than the
poem old blank

streets with
picturesque names
flaking flesh off their bones

*book two*

*with veryan weston*

**tessellations**

*for jennifer*          **for luthéal piano**
*pike*                      composition
*cobbing*

for improviser
'mostly
too quiet to be heard'

we hear her
dancing in
brussels / rustles

a brush of heels
on floor gushes
printing vibrant scrolls                    (2003
                                                        March
the clavecin                                   14)
stop out the quills
quiver zitherly

the tap with a clap
or slap falls into frenzied
pentatones the harpe-

tirée stop pulled free
felt drops to
strangle an octave & lift it

this          →          (mute)          (stone

↓)

moment                  (voice)          (mask

↓)

jennifer                (over)           (monument

flattens like a kiss
the floor raising itself
to choreograph its tesserae

modestly pianissimo her
strings do not vibrate
against the quills

*on kevin ayers*

                verviers vendredi
                14 march 20-
                03 un

ruly red floss sinewy
claw at microphone cough
under a spot astonished

eye of time white
trainers scuffed on edge
of platform silver drums

blue denim shirt half
open he turns indolence
into an art form life

style wisdom nodding
time towards the inter
mission silver sandals

(from his past) tapping
the rhythms out half in
love with ease with fame

coy he signals SPIRIT OF
66 *un petit café* hushed
half spoken beached in

land in textile rundown 2
8% unemployed verviers'
wage

slaves his mask is his
master still & he's the
master slave of cool he

raises the fender
like a glass at last
to do it again for half

joy of it
there's no
thing else to be done


*against my double*

in the café brel he handjobs
the tempo snappy strings &
vomiting brass his screeches

sticky patches inside egregious
lovers' trousers sweat-stains
from armpits of sobbing drunks

he collapses palms rank pools
of national feeling it's more
car crash than crescendo

collective delusion & delight

*book three*

*for matthieu fallaize*

in the café oulipien
the chef is a poet & he serves
white wine mussels in a

creamy chilli sauce in one shell nestles
a perfect crab moist speck beached
on your fingertip too small to

eat quite perfect if you
like this outcome go to table 7 if
you don't exit this poem now


*a beat back in tempo perhaps 2 beats back (mg)*

marvin gaye in the winter of my
childhood on ostende strand watches
grey sea lap over grey sand thin lamp

posts in line front slumbering hotels
comb the pricked wind that picks bone
& mind sex & soul voice & thought

through tight leather & fur his eyes
tired from making love & music
in a shoestring studio let us freeze

him a promenade statue to
the memory of comeback he
whispers *incroyable* (vamp

& fade)

*after a tray of chocolate slice crashes on the stairs*

becoming fire by water
by drugs by car crash by song by
man the blonde

in tight jeans hops
up to her barstool
to read *the artist's*

*ticklish nervous system*
*comes first with the news*
not fear

but hope
goes out of itself makes
people broad instead of

confining leaving she
heaves her limbs
across the boulevard

anspach a car
clips her toe-caps turning
thrown into

what is becoming
the impressability
of things aspirant

burning in motor fumes

## election day glance poems

form: glance
content: chance
_____
response: dance

vote for the one who
sings like an encrypted
lark arguments

as secret
as a house brick

vote for yourself

*


the zinc white of indecision
the ivory black of indecision
the burnt umber of indecision

*


vote for bigger recycling bins

amid booths & rubber
boxes with a voting
slip in one hand his

other held high to
be counted as soon
as the slip disappears

    two votes in
    one slit the
    gap between

her teeth as
she folds the
papers over

interest in him
wanes he's nothing
left to choose

\*

*the king is inviolable*
*his ministers accountable*
not party to this poem

ivy
fingering the
words birds

in the dripping trees
chirping like a call
centre with final pleading

vote for me

\*

the viridian of decision
the ultramarine of decision
the burnt sienna of decision

\*

clematis
clambering to the
top over re-

cycling men
fluorescent like disaster
workers crashing through rubble

     remember the firemen
     hosing government buildings
     clean as we mourned

     in white

\*

steaming bus of
students (first
time voters)

re-cycling lorry re-
versing lights
spinning

(politics)

scruffy woman
stuffing letter
boxes limp

flags
in the sodden
botanique

where no one
administers
the swans

(today)

\*

message to all liberals *if*

*you carry on putting crap*
*through my letterbox i'll*
*vote* vlaams belang

\*


the vermilion of undecision
the yellow ochre of undecision
the flake white of undecision

\*


windows open at
campaign hq
no signs of

life three point
turns at a political
crossroad the car

plastered with florid
ribbons flattened by rain
scours the avenue

# from *ovid's twistier & new amores*

*prelude*

fragile limbs naso
your three feathers fume
from helmet clamped

to burning head you
rear on your horse its
guernica

eyes teeth plait
-ed mane tail your
cloak flails flares

as you wing gladius
sword in one hand
mongrel iconography

hands you a severed wild
head you hold in the
other by wire hair

whose purple
body crouches
footstool-low

scratching native dirt your
shield shields you from
nothing

      wilder

           hooves
thunder across
ice a flash of
rage raiding sunless

tomis sundered
headstone thumbnail
out of dung

smouldering
plunder of your
molten resentments


## tristia bk 1: 7 the exiliad

*for phillipe thierry*

bin the press cuttings the imperial poetry prize
wipe the tapes of the olympiad the shaky video
of my north sea pinings for exilic marvin gaye dear

friend delete my emails defriend me on facebook
for every time you see my thumbnail
you'll weep & tweet

*how unhappy he must be forever off-line in the*
*valley of bad signal hard drive wiped the final*
*draft of* the book of ch-ch-ch-changes *deleted*

but i've kept a fair copy on pen-drive old friend & it
awaits my final tweaks but while
we're on the subject if you'll beg my pardon

(no i mean really *beg my pardon* did i not
explain the distinction between *relegatio &*
*exilium*?) that opus of mine (thank the odd

god or two that nicander is out of ©) could
remind you of me like the signet you wear
that bears my image but what i really want to say is

that book of the dead will survive unchanged my death
great friend: is there room in the rome that you roam in
for its twisted transpadane transformations?


*tristia bk 5: 7: the victimologist manifesto*

the sewage farm pumps
goldfish into the danube
good health *he writes*

mine!
as well as yours you'd
want it that way i

know you'd wish me well
& you'd like to know how
i'm doing *the voice*

*in the words unscrolls preens*
*a plume & says*
i'm stuffed! *as to a man*

*in a call centre in germania* (btw that
sythian muzak he played while he checked
my account with rome was crap)

oracular i rendered unto the great one
& he rent me asunder &
i resent (nothing

arresting in my account!) enough
of that! how'bout a bit
of gonzo journo rap? i can't

understand a word they say here
it's worse than antwerp their
poisonous contracts with immediate

effect big bellies beards wearing
black t-shirts bearing the legend
**HUNG LIKE EINSTEIN (brains**

**like donkeys)** they limp
into the bar for watery
kriek *he cries* stuck here

while my imperial service in verse
is forgotten my scrolls bound tight
to beat slaves (no doubt)....

*this victim is famous for*
*being a victim they*
*applaud his pantomimes back*

*home as he sits in his shit & sings*
'what does not differ is indifference/
forgive me muses/i'm

not the one who
chooses' *dear naso*
*i've a scriptorium*

*scratching out scrolls*
*by the lisping adriatic i wonder if you'd care*
*to send me a skinful a bit more* **a-**

**more** *please do it like dean martin does*
*artificial effortless*
*& with whinging & whining off stage*

*new amores bk 1: 5*

into summer afternoon heat
of our shuttered crepuscule
you enter slip

tensible straps down
cleaving silk upon
sheeny stockings

tensing your back
against me you
hold back

halfmoon bra falls
in half-darkness &
i turn with moistened

lips musky fingers for em-
passioned meat deep below
your perfect slopes with

cavernous tang sucked
tongue & your lick-
spittle sphinx smile

you shudder
release re-
joice & relax!

until we're complete & i
fall apart exiled shade
twinned in twilight for jove

knows tangled hair & cleft
flesh
*must return to roma-*

ny scarf & sensible skirt as
your high heels & tight lips
carry off my wanton verses

        each evening you absorb
        applause for
        persistence from your

        husband lukewarm
        like a courtesan
        before supper all

night he guards your shallow
moat with his rubber sword
dry as a bone in its defence

*new amores bk 1:16   joyful cruelty*

unseen
      licking
            i pull
the pearls of
your nipples as you

milk a moan churning
your dun perspirant body your
finger turning

into your self
& turning passion out
like a startled foal

a hoof-kick in-
side the guts shuddering
down & out hair

flows around your hot
face in the fan sticks across
your flush smiling cheeks

as you refocus & catch me
unworded in your deep
pools but in-forming i

slap your face until
your cheek
flames your lip swells

      i come into your eyes
      until your vision
      of me stings

*residues*

*... un golpe de objetos*
—Neruda

1 *party*

between be-
tween &
beyond eye

lost voice apologises
for its loss this obdurate
thing seen this object this

plump pillow
of blood
abject this

poem apologises
for the 'holocaust
of objects' after

the bottle party orgy
of displaced places
a chair where a child now

swings his legs drinking milk
on which his mother (last night) swelled
for neighbourly lens in sperm-

shot nurture &
its eye sucked
her sebacious breasts

partly
apart a
part of reality

broken loose
loose &
broken

                    voice
            bottle   child
              chair  leg


2

it
all
spills

spins
torques dis-
placed splayed

displayed products
& services one arthritic click prickling at the pores
delivers the plump palette to your apartment your voice

do you conserve shadowy cupboards to fill with dust?
do you fall to gnawing leg of lamb raw frozen poisonous
sausage of offal venison veal tripe trotter partridge duckling quail

not with style masquerading as civilisation
terminal designs by the antwerp six stumbling
on a cat walk or an eternally astonished

saviour child roasting under glass at the place du jeu de balle
teeming with junk panoptic
pyramids flecking the horizon with dust in the eye tele-

scopes antlers coffeepots chairlegs gramophones
vases sweet-jars fashion function durable trash
& funk scrum spitting over offcuts oddbins ragbags … ?

## 3 *entropoetics (drafts of critique)*

*one*

recorded crisp on magnetic
tape fades as it replays
into a basso mumble blur

*two*

sucking wet unspeaking
sucked dry softened
nipple-apple

*three*

as it leans creaks sinks
as weight shifts predicts futurity
as soft-splintering collapse

# english dust: homage to jeff keen

            threaten
the handheld war shudders
loose-frame domestics
to a sound-track of

screeching nails
with old film stock singeing
as it's projected
            direct

with acid stencils drawing
                masks
on second screen
junk skips tipped im-

ploded cinema test
acuity with this limit
case of blacked out ballet
        forms

                test
the viewer lifted
from voice-over fleeting
milky rim bared breast in a car wreck

bleached screen throws you
snowblind as south coast super-
            heroes
emerge from littoral blizzard

as they might in sub-
zero developing fluid
                buckled
doubled flattened

torn spotted blotted
streaked stained
     mottled
soaked burnt &

        reversed:
pure flash
cartoons of glance
flick speckle

▲

ode

to an emoticon winking freshly on a spit-spattered screen
like this poem a face opens
the container is all too full of itself

click onto it & it links (itself) to another point in the process
eternal to the moment when the corporation pulls the plug
& the page pastes its blank message upon the desire that eulogises

at a quarter to nine every morning i hear the factory siren
but there is no factory in this district it is itself
manufacturing the idea of manufacturing without euphony

the object before us on the screen is not the screen
we cannot pick it free like a splinter in the flesh
(it is not in it or behind or in other micro-metaphors)

it is deleting itself eternally on a frozen screen as the battery swoons
it is threatening to turn into something i must mourn
while offering me nothing that majestically restores down to less


▲

elegy

the evocation of the body that will never re-materialise
the desire for the speech of the body that will never etc
this tracing of the loved one is the love

the face opening blushes her smile floats free
the face opening forever as the chances close
the face opening & closing like a swinging door

the face covered with blotches a smile fights free
the face covered with scratches from the scrapping
the face covered with lipstick slapped by imaginary mouths

the face that is forgotten pore by pore scar by scar
like a photoshopped image purified at each click
drained of detail drenched with light as

spectral as a badly varnished freshly scraped old master
this is where i am meant to venerate vulnerability in my self
by pledging all my desire to backspace deleting absence

but this is the place where i drag & drop my self
in a soundfile of scavenger gulls swooping low over the city crying
an elegy to their mute monumental appetites


▲


poetics

the poem that is
*au sujet de au sujet de*
the matter that forms the

forms that matter this
tracing of the poem
is the poem

the poem opens
nothing &
that settles it (& us)

that's something at least
what the shaping thinks
what the soundings think

what the words do not think
as they rattle around the mind
making a racket we

do not think & just as we
are ready to go
it offers a making

we cannot resist
the vintage tin in the loft
containing the relic we cannot

see the ashes that will never
glow again a beloved
consuming object that rustles

it is the poem entire & shut & open

*cow 1*

under a confection of fucked chandeliers

the queen of shoes has polish tins
laid out their angel wings flicked open
to absorb & absolve the princess's secret sin

she whispers in the dark jockey's ear
graffiti she reads from palace walls blooming
speech bubbles with embellished tags

puncturing rather than punctuating
her obscene verses the witnesses' rictal
incontinence betrays it's a dirty one

a veil like a vapour laughs blankets
their language-centres
this pure explosion of fuck-you poetry:

       there was a young princess called madoc
       whose dead dowager smelt like a haddock
              by royal ascent
              or by mankind's descent
       she was filleted in the horses' paddock

(17 minutes)

*cow 4*

will our melancholy daughters
live as long as darwin's tortoise
in this new century of slaughters

when like its own rebuttal
the space shuttle
is a subtle

closing chapter of one such history
what mystery
is now slapped on my story

like the fresh silver paint on the bathroom cupboard
that stands drying on the landing which once harboured
your potions to port & my germoloids to starboard

i'm a bath-tub sailor
as the day grows paler
awash with weeping adrift on failure

a crusoe of verse a sacrificial ovid
flattened of ego & of id
delivered walking wounded from dante horrid

in fecal decay i scratch these frenchy tercets
& with my dribbling bladder of percepts
i piss these poems on your thingy concepts


(8 minutes)

# Flemish Poems

*translated by Martin Krol*

# Untitled

*after poems by Herman de Coninck and Roland Jooris*

Shrivelled black pants
lie strewn about the poem
the dusty gully by her bed

set in syntax where they dropped
impossible heels keeled over
what do you think these things

the window beyond this shivering blind
overlooks a blind wall call it real
whatever the rude world offers

she peeps out naked from behind it
by looking in you're looking out.

# Four Sides

*after Guillevic*

## 1

The day begins quite
precisely like a right angle
struck in the air like an angel's
fist, leaving
a nagging debt to the world,
that perfect circle with no centre.
Shield. Coin. Pay tribute
to its demands
that flex like a triangle
trying to add up to 366 degrees,
until it breaks, incommensurable.

The equilateral of love.

## 2

Fleet clouds low over the flatlands
of Flanders, all that phlegm
in our voices, coughing up
cigarette laughter and alliteration,
all that stuff that won't do any more.

A dot at circle's centre
we think ourselves
out on this plane where the cows
cower under fibrous grey.

No melody this morning. Think rather
we're crushed into the armpit
of a trapezoid
waiting for the figure
to collapse,

for this plane to shrink
to a sphincter.


3


One is thinking a sinusoid
in the cage of a parallelepiped
snaking against the fluxing bars,
giddy with possibility. One
turns oneself inside out

at the phone.

One looks out at puddles
dotted with rain.
Waveforms of circular intent
spread and interfuse

under the ghostly procession
of cloud under cloud,

a solid sky that can't be turned,
but presses down on one
as one stumps across the field
to the canal's line, one's thoughts
at a tangent.


4


The day clears, sinks exhausted
under skullcap sky and crescent
moon. I expire with it, a
line retracting into a point the

point erased

# The Light

Break open the light, the light
that lifts like an airship at dawn,
that grows to fill the sky, the morning sky,
translucent and floating like hope,
break open the sky, a vapour,
gaseous light broken open on a cloud, a perforated cloud,
fretful and low, break open the clouds,
their torn edges, turning,
until a pool breaks, a silver pool breaks open, shreds its banks, rifts,
and sunlight pours through golden and burning
(that circle on the eye, breaking as we look away, the circle
fading in the eye), break open the sun, the sly sun,
dripping its reflection on the bonnet of the car, bonnet
shimmering from a shower earlier, break open the shower,
the fine rain breaking on the sheen of the tarmac, glowing
silver, break open the car, but not like a thief,
wrench its roof off like a tin, the roof of the car,
peel it back to inspect ambulatory pleasures of
map and radio, break open the radio, spill its
circuitry like teeth from a mouth urging, urgent,
the sky's own life generalised to a kind of news there,
a blank summary without density or weight,
break open the voice into flurries of sound,
white noise in a snow blizzard, break open the road, the pavement,
the manholes, the bollards, the flood-drains,
come then, break open the gate, the whorled cast-iron gate,
vibrating on its hinges, rusted or oiled, crude
gamelan, break open its vibrations, the gate-latch
trembling for fingertips, ah! human, you appear at last
human, though seldom placed there for such a purpose,
any purpose, even waiting at the end of the path, waiting even
for a purpose, at the gate that opens onto the path, the path
you hesitate before, break open the purpose, break open
the human purpose, the seldom-placed fingers,
not cracking them like a twig, like that, not like that,

break everything open with no pain, break them
open, the open fingers, like a break in cloud again,
break open the finger made of cloud pointing
to its own dispersal, a tendril shaping forever un-
shaping in morphologies of distension,
drifting in leisurely haste, cloud
that was a finger, a 'finger of cloud'
as the breakfast weather report reports, break
open the shapes you see there, breaking like news, horse-
head, archipelago, vagina, ragged sponge soaked
with weighty filth, fists of angry air sculpted
by your eye, break open the eye, the open eye,
spill its residue of vision, vitreous, the things
you never see, lost in your looking, the plenitude
that tumbles like an evening wrecking the afternoon, break
open all vision, all things unseen, the light that is
and the light that isn't, break open the map at last
as it unfolds on the lap of the lost traveller
while sky lifts away to leave unbroken slate.

# Here and Where

The tomcat's whiskers brush across my cheek.
His purring pours into my dream this buzzing,
the faulty fridge from which I stole rancid milk
after sleeping all night on your sofa.
The day distances itself from the dream,
courts business-like denials of responsibility.
Jet trails, tight grey wisps against a silver sky
are purloined by rooftops. A lozenge of haze
rolls over on the sun behind the chimneystack.
Cauliflower clouds clench their watery fists.
The trails, as I watch them, sink
from their freezing meridian, turn to

worn guts      worm casts      warm fur


Where? where a beard of wires hangs in
the gloves of a terrorist, where
daisies nip your ankles as you skip
towards me under the city's hatbox skyline,
where disappointment follows our appointment
by the fountain, where the sky itself
throws its crystal image of you

against the glacier


The sun fights through the sky's deepening oppression,
grey glove across its mouth. It sings
a muffled ballad of illimitable truth. The uniforms
call for reinforcements, measures: the shot in the arm,
bequeathing a mogadon sky to a monotone day.
I settle under my collar, wait for real weather,

expecting the worst (who said truth, who said real?).
I see infinite gradations in the heavens' degradations:

abstractions of zebra, multiples of zero

# He feels the bell…

He feels the bell
of silence encasing him,
ringing hard, a dream
of clamour. He hears
the rain beyond that,
bubbling in gutters,
grumbling down pipes,
to storm-drains, ditches,
excited disputations of day
in a language he doesn't.
Not certain whether he's
drowning or sinking in
arguments contrasting
privileged delight
to habitual nightmare,
and not certain whether one
isn't turning into the other,
without warning
he surfaces like a diver
with the bends through what
could be a skein
of throbbing, thrombose,
his eyes opening on
rolling Alaskas of cloud
breasting Arctic oceans
in membranous sky beyond

beyond everything but yearning

# The Word

*We are an echo of an echo of the sky.*
—Jaan Kaplinski

Sky.
Sky the hue of a sick egg unbroken.
A half-formed beak. Talons clawing at fog. Mottled rug
flung over the furniture of day. A chair leg's betrayal.
Everything out of place. The sky could go on
displaying itself forever like this. Flaking
immeasurably. I could go on describing it forever.
Verbing its adjectival noun adverbally. Stop. The poem
could go on forever. It tells us the best way
of going on. Go. On forever turn the sky into something else
a semblance of itself the poem's. A fish winching
itself across a screen of smudged clarities.
It's taking place in the spaces of the poem.
Smoke for blocked chimneys. Shallows of blue
in the depths open up. Like the poem. Atlas
dictionary thesaurus tugging at my sleeve.
A spasm across a keyboard. I've not used the word yet.
The word underlined in every draft you reject.
The word that rides the tongue. A tongue riding
the word is the word. Moistening the sky it forms.
Anything that enters the sky is the sky.
Anything that enters the poem is the poem.

# Ballerina

She wears the same slip in this poem too
You remember her avatar wore it before her
in fictions that recoiled from the frisson
of unceasing rain and which
stopped mid-sentence when they
stepped from the arcade into a shower
flung down like a challenge
Initial touching led to the designated place
where he came copiously into her cupped palms
She poured it from hand to hand like a proposition
evenly balanced between here and now
She wears the same slip in this poem too and
passion already snakes over her shoulder
and rolls down the curve of her back
where my hands follow smoothing a path
She shifts under the slip breasts shake free
We're programmed for controlled mania
She delivers herself on moist fingertips
She comes out from her spaces to fill the place she fills
I spin her around like a ballerina
on a music box and drop to the floor
She no longer wears the slip in this poem
I enter her pressing against the pushing
feeling for the secret seal of her body
I enter her and her body fills with the spaces beyond
Pushing as she pulls pulled back as I
accept all kisses from her from the world
that watches us from the shadows we make
its phantom hot hand touching my back
My shadow pumps her shadow until
I flatten like flaming oil hitting a spillage

# Lyric

This
looks      like      with   no                           the poem
nothing   the world        one   write                   that is
        I love            to      it     lifting        left
                                            nothing but


carried     from
           nowhere    on                         no
                     a wind       that cries
                                               name



           silence emptied of silence

                     clouds fray
                     sky floats free I


                                       cannot entune
cannot                                 friable
release           cannot            blossom
the word         entwine
               waxen leaves

# Manifest (constellation)

| | | | |
|---|---|---|---|
| sacrifice | bow your head | | inked |
| your words | to the earth | the night sky | (with) |
| to air | | | gravity |
| | | | |
| the Under- | space | from | beneath |
| world is no | forms | which | the pyramid |
| lighter | the bridge | you | |
| | | | |
| | | drop | |
| | | | |
| wisdom | | time | on the surface |
| | the labyrinth | entwines | |
| and all that | enfolds | space | |
| | | | |
| site | poetry | the tips | we read |
| is | | of mountain | the |
| vertical | specific | touch the stars | constellations |

# In this room

*i.m. Guy Mees*

In this room the floor is white. There's nothing more to be said of it, huge tile, levelled grave. The ceiling is black. Stretching starless. Chess squares with no pieces, no moves.

Four walls also square. You've entered this space. Or the space has entered you. You're not making this up; it's making you. You're inside this cube. But nothing supports you. You hang at centre point, though you have no sensation of flying, floating or falling. You carry your coordinates like a dream. It is a space with no place.

The walls are blank, colourless though not white. You examine their surfaces for the hint of a door, a handle, keyhole – even hairline crack of a window, a slit, spyhole. There's nothing. You have no idea how you got here; you've no idea how you will escape, if the act of leaving is escape. You have little memory of before, and mere fizzles of expectation.

As time passes, ectoplasmic phantoms resolve on the walls. Like the glimmer of film projected in daylight. Or like the reflection of a flock of geese flickering on the inside of your spectacles as it passes across your bent head, an overcast autumn morning imported from the banks of the Schelde.

Your mind, in its isolation, concentrates into this act of looking. You're less sure about yourself the more there is to read. What unfolds is a ghostly transaction with history conducted in sepulchral cities and by glassy canals. A world prematurely grey, unreadable: mouth shapes in city fog or country mist, sign language in fur.

You don't notice at first that the ceiling has blanched, a pearl cloud without break or height. Or that the floor blackens to a pool both shallow and deep. Its swart surface shines over invisible viscosity, impenetrable light.

Only in this room do black and white make sense.

# Roomstanzas:
## Quennets for Floor, 4 Walls and Ceiling

echoic steps

blinding darkness
noctiphobic business

winding staircase

cement leisure

damp thinking
living wage

living space

hedonistic vault

sybaritic crypt
glass cube

echoic basement

You're that
little girl told
to drop down the cellar
to collect potatoes
which rattled across the floor
like rats hairy and dirty
and coal blacker than night

vomit bunker

winding darkness
interrupted night

nyctophobic light

| sunken chair | raised eyebrows | hazardous rug |
| | irredeemable space | |
| polished tables | tarnished medals | stone owls |
| | spotless spots | |
| stuffed boxfiles | dusty pockets | yellowing bills |
| | greasy glasses | |

Ghosts of the living
haunt the
air filled
with the peppery motes
of 20000
TV sessions and 50
old new years

| spotless owls | irredeemable bills | incomprehensible certificates |
| | empty wills | |

boxed spoons      chemical washing-machine      carcinogenic bubbles

rattling knives

obsolete beans      cankerous pickles      tupperware salt

vinegar fly

grieving pegs      poisonous medicines      boxed receipts

glass knives

Only the fridge hums
like a happy cook
In the cupboards utensils
and their deputies await
the attrition of wear and
tear 5 dustpans
6 brushes

lizard life      personalised mugs      silver spoons

bleached pepper

| pillaged tie-rack | broken jewel | incomprehensible weather |
| | spittle tissue | |
| astonished ring | fossil blossoms | breathless windows |
| | medicine glue | |
| esturine geese | flaming turret | sempiternal infancy |
| | glass eye | |

Pillows like sandbags
stacked against 10000 dreams
Curtains drawn on
curtains baffle the day
Tallboys of suitcases
for the trip to nowhere rain-
coats that will never moisten


| amaranthine corruption | eolian coat-hanger | aeonian summer |
| | incorruptible earpiece | |

spineless spines

unpoetic poems
fossil coins

sleepless bed

another world

wordless pages
newsprint fur

yellow ceiling

martian plaything

finger dust
printed glass

footless footprint

Library for sleepers
museum of
adolescence
A pile of 78s
caught in the bowed palm
of 30 years' silence
Ships idle on the tide

fleeting capitals

floating jewel
fossil joy

irredeemable damp

| | | |
|---|---|---|
| *winding staircase* | *blinding darkness* | *muted commerce* |
| | *paddling windmill* | |
| *sloped circulation* | *padded interruption* | *nyctohylophobic timbers* |
| | *lordly garret* | |
| *graceful attic* | *papyrus penthouse* | *walrus carcass* |
| | *glass cube* | |

*You're that little boy*
*told to climb into*
*the loft to collect presents*
*who found the porno mag saw*
*hairy buttocks*
*pumping a black woman*
*mouth open like a tunnel*

| | | |
|---|---|---|
| *blinding staircase* | *negrophillic frenzy* | *ecstatic summit* |
| | *nephophobic chimmeypots* | |

[macroversion for the interior of a room
microversion for the inside of a folded paper cube
performance version for empty space]

# Call this room

*after Michalis Pichler*

Call this room the memory room.

Build it from space, in space: floor walls roof.

Peripheral light on the central eclipse – that's you.

No trapdoor, no stepladder, but a geometry of affect. Avoid the pinch of the cube.

Borrow this room from the Museum of Amnesia, they'll not miss it. The exhibition that bears your name is postponed.

Space flows around the thing, mind adheres to the noun.

Something is born in this room, along with its name.

It is a book, shut. Black book on white lectern.

Open it. Words rise like locusts. They hang in vapours, breathing, pitting the air. Collect as constellations. Freeze.

As you move through the room the constellations change configuration. What was shipwreck flat on the page is the ocean itself in three dimensions. What was word becomes shape. Call it 'poem', call it 'image'. Then call it 'sculpture'.

Call it the memory room.

In what sense is it a room, invaded as it is with flecks of artifice, frozen confetti showers? It winks hints on how to move artfully, though not gracefully, through it.

The walls fill with images flickering for recognition: the frosty spires in a valley, the stepped roofs of the Toll Collector's house, the Torengebouw's modernist angles mocking the fog that attempts to soften them. Your singular ones.

The room calls you to perform your presence here.

You are composed of these dimensions and of the things that haunt them.

It all depends on how you see them, black or white, muddied with colour, or as Perspex words hanging from wires, as you weave between, trying to find the one point where it all makes sense. You were promised this, but you can't find it. You say:

'The room calls me to perform my disappearance.'

Read in the dark: black image making light.

# In the Complex

*I*

a    If I crackle his feathers will he sell me a ticket to Brussels Central?

b    When you enter the cage all the seats are taken by lizard-spotters clicking to themselves.

c    Where we gather beneath the booming dome, which bounces destinations around its bowl, elephants trumpet in bronchial triumph.

d    Whomsoever he meets at the railings greets him with shrieks, howls, hissing through bared teeth, and a dancing display that may not be described in polite company (which is where you sit at last on a seat made of sighs).

e    How she got here, with the sort of sneeze that flattens the commuter crowd like a corn-circle, is not clear.

f    What they think about, waiting at the barriers, is the re-tinted movie, the one where the Ape Man knifes a rubber rhino to the overdub of his war-cry.

*II*

a    What I really want I can really have amid this sea-breeze air-con: a new kind of cereal or a perfumed enema, a bath that cleanses me while I'm asleep, an e-biography of the man who had the ex-prime minister's love-child, etc....

b    If you're wheeling between the aisles, sniffing the organics, squeezing the plastics, tapping the minerals, don't be alarmed if you're 'apprehended' as the 'anything suspicious' conjured by the metallic voice aloft.

c    When we were young we had capacious nostrils, abysmal throats and curling ears. Now we've piggy eyes, fly-zip lips and pyramids of tins to play like xylophones on electronic consoles.

d    Where he darts behind the marble slab, amid the cosmetic ambrosia of uniformed girls, he dispenses drugs like samples of coral.

e    Who she thinks she is she can become, applying gloopy barbeque sauce to her arms with sausage fingers, disguised as the aroma of bad diet that air freshener will disperse with pineapple trace.

f    How they deal with waste, taint, discharge, checkout, etc....

*III*

a    How I got here. By physical examination, by spiritual inebriation. By my forebears' ability to perform tricks with bottles like warring clowns.

b    What you bring to the table. A tight rubber hose, crisp with hops. Platonic shapes fashioned from glass.

c    If we race to empty this barrel they'll be another (and another!) and we'll still be the milk monitors: we're the tallest boys in Europe!

d    When he wins the prize it evaporates at his touch. Like the touch of his touch.

e    Where she stands in the corridor she can smell the bubbles cooking in the laboratory below. She knows that only the spherical ones will rate red ticks on the clipboard. The rest released to the jumping cats.

f    Who they think they are at any moment dictates the labels they select for each bomb they make. Trial and error.

*IV*

a    Who I see brushed up here is a frock-coated manufacturer from the Era of Colonial Trade, stuck on a crumbled plinth and plastered with a colour called Illusion.

b    How you got here may have to do with the pellets that the ancient machine spits into the overflowing bucket at your feet marked EMPTY.

c    What we want under these cornices are images of the past brought to life and knocked up into modern semblance at the doable rate of one per hour.

d    If he were to wear the sugared lilac uniform he might become invisible, staring all day at the hammer striking the anvil, the sharp chips of its blows.

e    When she poses for the mould of Psyche everybody watches as though she's turned to a jasmine shimmer, become venerable like the past, though it's our business to manufacture the future. Or is it the other way round in those palace mirrors that catch her milky curves as cascades of warping light?

f    Where they gather by the revolving door, they acquire new thoughts, of communal wisdom and of collective control, of rights denied. Thoughts that they are no longer making up the past. They're starting to make trouble.

*V*

a Where I peer into the microscope the edges of the coin are empiricals, empires assigned to confidential waste, micro-dynasties elected to collective guilt.

b Who you want to become is god, or at least his eye on the fake dollar bill, as you blush to admit that you still practise alchemy among so much humming lilac echo plastic and under custom-designed low-lit pre-fabricated ceilings.

c How we track down the forger and trick him into exchanging a casket of nail-clipping epithelials from the Myrmidons' spear-feast should provide plot enough for series 12 episode 21.

d What he does is essential but incommensurable, he whispers.

e If she is guilty then she can follow the evidence and re-calibrate the proportion of gold to base metal on-screen.

f When they inspect the matrix they find a spider—black speck with shrivelled crushed legs—minted onto the emperor's face a thousand times. They'll either have to melt the whole batch down or touch up his online identikit with a squashed arachnid tattoo.

*VI*

a     'When I was a revolutionist I was interrogated in this very room!' I boom into the microphone that regards me like a guard, like the guard of a guard.

b     Where you are holed-up now is a radio studio broadcasting your (fake) prison diaries to rouse the populace still suffering 'under the Nazis and their Black Walloon running dogs'.

c     Who we want to become are dummies in the Museum of Amnesia, you know, the ones that demonstrate deprivation and all that stuff.

d     How he escaped was preserved as the sound of scraping brick and sifting sand that later became the national anthem.

e     What she presides over is black tea, thick and acidic.

f     If they catch the ex-prime minister, they could reproduce his prison as a tent of silence. Not a word would escape.

You flee the Complex, slip through the folds between permutations one night.

You see it for what it is at last: the surface cap of a half-abandoned nuclear silo, a contaminated business estate. A nursery of follies in a decommissioned enterprise zone. An occult science park.

Stiff necked surveillance cameras twist to watch you go. Past bulldozed libraries, museums and art galleries: plaster dust, asbestos flour, acrylic fumes.

The bridge from the island tunnels into the night, the spot-lit gantries beating the pulse of an unknown language as you cross.

You turn to see the units' white fangs biting the curved neck of the corniche.

Just by looking you are turning mist into sails in the Marina. You transform darkness into sound, the clouds breaking into sonatas that shield humankind from the cacophony of everything in sight, everything at once.

[The units of the complex may be assembled in at least two fashions, each of 6 parts; one, by reading each unit as printed here (I-VI (a-f)), secondly by reading each corresponding line a-f across sections I-VI. The coda (in **bold**) remains integral for both readings. More adventurous readers might apply Mathews's Algorithm to the units to obtain advanced re-assembly of the complex.]

# Revolutionary Song

*after Bill Viola*

the lone Fiat on the boulevard dissolves the crack
lone Fiat on the boulevard dissolves the crack of
Fiat on the boulevard dissolves the crack of thunder
on the boulevard dissolves the crack of thunder sounds
the boulevard dissolves the crack of thunder sounds like
boulevard dissolves the crack of thunder sounds like bricks
dissolves the crack of thunder sounds like bricks crashing
the crack of thunder sounds like bricks crashing birds
crack of thunder sounds like bricks crashing birds fleeing
of thunder sounds like bricks crashing birds fleeing the
thunder sounds like bricks crashing birds fleeing the sky
sounds like bricks crashing birds fleeing the sky dissolve

like bricks crashing birds fleeing the sky dissolve pearl-grey
bricks crashing birds fleeing the sky dissolve pearl-grey streaks
crashing birds fleeing the sky dissolve pearl-grey streaks caught
birds fleeing the sky dissolve pearl-grey streaks caught in
fleeing the sky dissolve pearl-grey streaks caught in sunlight
the sky dissolve pearl-grey streaks caught in sunlight the
sky dissolve pearl-grey streaks caught in sunlight the bleeding
dissolve pearl-grey streaks caught in sunlight the bleeding man
pearl-grey streaks caught in sunlight the bleeding man strung
streaks caught in sunlight the bleeding man strung up
caught in sunlight the bleeding man strung up in
in sunlight the bleeding man strung up in the
sunlight the bleeding man strung up in the tree
the bleeding man strung up in the tree dissolves

bleeding man strung up in the tree dissolves the
man strung up in the tree dissolves the banker
strung up in the tree dissolves the banker deliberately
up in the tree dissolves the banker deliberately looks
in the tree dissolves the banker deliberately looks bored

the tree dissolves the banker deliberately looks bored at
tree dissolves the banker deliberately looks bored at his
dissolves the banker deliberately looks bored at his trial
the banker deliberately looks bored at his trial the
banker deliberately looks bored at his trial the abandoned
deliberately looks bored at his trial the abandoned car
looks bored at his trial the abandoned car by
bored at his trial the abandoned car by the
at his trial the abandoned car by the lighthouse
his trial the abandoned car by the lighthouse dissolves

trial the abandoned car by the lighthouse dissolves the
the abandoned car by the lighthouse dissolves the Magic
abandoned car by the lighthouse dissolves the Magic Muslim
car by the lighthouse dissolves the Magic Muslim walks
by the lighthouse dissolves the Magic Muslim walks by
the lighthouse dissolves the Magic Muslim walks by the
lighthouse dissolves the Magic Muslim walks by the sandbags
dissolves the Magic Muslim walks by the sandbags the
the Magic Muslim walks by the sandbags the framed
Magic Muslim walks by the sandbags the framed photograph
Muslim walks by the sandbags the framed photograph of
walks by the sandbags the framed photograph of victims
by the sandbags the framed photograph of victims dissolves

the sandbags the framed photograph of victims dissolves the
sandbags the framed photograph of victims dissolves the slick
the framed photograph of victims dissolves the slick pornography
framed photograph of victims dissolves the slick pornography of
photograph of victims dissolves the slick pornography of stainless
of victims dissolves the slick pornography of stainless steel
victims dissolves the slick pornography of stainless steel glints
dissolves the slick pornography of stainless steel glints the
the slick pornography of stainless steel glints the spangled
slick pornography of stainless steel glints the spangled acrobats
pornography of stainless steel glints the spangled acrobats in
of stainless steel glints the spangled acrobats in mid-air
stainless steel glints the spangled acrobats in mid-air dissolve

steel glints the spangled acrobats in mid-air dissolve the
glints the spangled acrobats in mid-air dissolve the packing
the spangled acrobats in mid-air dissolve the packing case
spangled acrobats in mid-air dissolve the packing case tower
acrobats in mid-air dissolve the packing case tower blocks
in mid-air dissolve the packing case tower blocks rear
mid-air dissolve the packing case tower blocks rear up
dissolve the packing case tower blocks rear up at
the packing case tower blocks rear up at the
packing case tower blocks rear up at the day
case tower blocks rear up at the day blindfolded
tower blocks rear up at the day blindfolded men
blocks rear up at the day blindfolded men in
rear up at the day blindfolded men in dark
up at the day blindfolded men in dark cells
at the day blindfolded men in dark cells dissolve

the day blindfolded men in dark cells dissolve thunder
day blindfolded men in dark cells dissolve thunder vomits
blindfolded men in dark cells dissolve thunder vomits behind
men in dark cells dissolve thunder vomits behind the
in dark cells dissolve thunder vomits behind the screen
dark cells dissolve thunder vomits behind the screen of
cells dissolve thunder vomits behind the screen of rain
dissolve thunder vomits behind the screen of rain her
thunder vomits behind the screen of rain her curved
vomits behind the screen of rain her curved back
behind the screen of rain her curved back as
the screen of rain her curved back as she
screen of rain her curved back as she stoops
of rain her curved back as she stoops for
rain her curved back as she stoops for the
her curved back as she stoops for the bath
curved back as she stoops for the bath towel
back as she stoops for the bath towel dissolves

as she stoops for the bath towel dissolves blood
she stoops for the bath towel dissolves blood covers

stoops for the bath towel dissolves blood covers the
for the bath towel dissolves blood covers the priest's
the bath towel dissolves blood covers the priest's fresh
bath towel dissolves blood covers the priest's fresh surplice
towel dissolves blood covers the priest's fresh surplice the
dissolves blood covers the priest's fresh surplice the blush
blood covers the priest's fresh surplice the blush of
covers the priest's fresh surplice the blush of the
the priest's fresh surplice the blush of the winning
priest's fresh surplice the blush of the winning beauty
fresh surplice the blush of the winning beauty queen
surplice the blush of the winning beauty queen dissolves

the blush of the winning beauty queen dissolves independence
blush of the winning beauty queen dissolves independence is
of the winning beauty queen dissolves independence is declared
the winning beauty queen dissolves independence is declared in
winning beauty queen dissolves independence is declared in the
beauty queen dissolves independence is declared in the regions
queen dissolves independence is declared in the regions the
dissolves independence is declared in the regions the leashed
independence is declared in the regions the leashed dog
is declared in the regions the leashed dog on
declared in the regions the leashed dog on its
in the regions the leashed dog on its walk
the regions the leashed dog on its walk dissolves

regions the leashed dog on its walk dissolves the
the leashed dog on its walk dissolves the melodious
leashed dog on its walk dissolves the melodious pissoir
dog on its walk dissolves the melodious pissoir of
on its walk dissolves the melodious pissoir of Ste-Catherine
its walk dissolves the melodious pissoir of Ste-Catherine sings
walk dissolves the melodious pissoir of Ste-Catherine sings walls
dissolves the melodious pissoir of Ste-Catherine sings walls of
the melodious pissoir of Ste-Catherine sings walls of butterflies
melodious pissoir of Ste-Catherine sings walls of butterflies dissolve

pissoir of Ste-Catherine sings walls of butterflies dissolve rain
of Ste-Catherine sings walls of butterflies dissolve rain settles
Ste-Catherine sings walls of butterflies dissolve rain settles into
sings walls of butterflies dissolve rain settles into the
walls of butterflies dissolve rain settles into the easiest
of butterflies dissolve rain settles into the easiest option
butterflies dissolve rain settles into the easiest option the
dissolve rain settles into the easiest option the gushing
rain settles into the easiest option the gushing eaves
settles into the easiest option the gushing eaves of
into the easiest option the gushing eaves of tomorrow
the easiest option the gushing eaves of tomorrow dissolve

# Ode to Orbit

*Vanaf het perron*
*waar wij allen stonden…*
　　　　　—Remco Campert

*On the Trans-Historical Railway*
　　*we could traffic you know*
*what with Cendras or arm-wrestle*
　　　　*with Álvaro de Campos*
　　　　　　—Maarten De Zoete

'Are we really a long way from Halle-Vilvoorde?'
Asks Gisele on the platform of this suburban station
Set on the track stretching homeward to the horizon and from it
We see the speck of the headlight of an approaching train
Dwindling and pulsing (it seems) a white dwarf
We feel the excitement of flight (O! the emerald mountains the
Meconium gorges of the Moon!)[1] and the relief of return (O!
Bunting in the streets spongy astroturf for the horses!) in one
Metallic distant sunflash perhaps two commuter stops off
Gisele who carries only her name as cargo (what is she a
Gynoid?) pushes against my arm in a caress oddly feline
For one second I know that we are dreaming
That I'm passing through lives that aren't mine a tunnel of arousal
Until I'm gasping in the sunheat of my apartment
In Ghent (where I have never lived!) waking my mouth
Full of blood I've sucked from my wounded tongues
And Gisele's nudging at my elbow becomes the cat pressing his old head
Heavy against me hungry for morning fish as he senses my re-entry to his
World and I tumble in airless sheets a pantomimic cyborg
Gisele's voice asking me again in the poem that crackles through my cells
'Are we really a long way from Halle-Vilvoorde?' I wake from
Interstellar daze to find my self strapped to a seat
In the feverish cabin of the oldest space station in orbit
The Third Fleming in Space my mouth full of the bitterness of separation
My cortex longs for a grimy glass of flat Orval in the dingiest of restaurants

Spilling the juice of the dodgiest of unyielding clams down my chin
Watching my self on the bartop TV flickering with static screen caked with
        grease
Taking my scripted slo-mo space walk wielding the largest pair of pliers
To fix a loose bolt in the flexing mineral skin while the curved Congo
Turns under above beyond me green and secretive seconds until
The Incident—the slashed EVA suit snagged on silence—and now
Dreams are narrative space junk orbiting the mind
Dropping a spanner yesterday and here it returns at fatal speed until
I'm awake in every place I've been and in all the others I haven't

      I'm standing (at least)
      on grey winter sands
      at Knokke (in black

      and white) with two school-friends Johannes
      Kemp (who will father children
      in middle age)

      and Gerrit Reeck (who will die a meaningless death at 17
      playing football beside the tramway at De Haan freak
      blood poisoning kick in the shin)

      and yet somehow
      I ride the cream trams at Knokke again
      fix them shakily in photographs (that half-preserve

      yet half-steal the memory from me which
      isn't mine or mine
      alone) and I'm back when I was still young

Waiting in the vomit-comet's padded cell to drop my first Zero G
My weight falls away like virginity from orgasm
As my personhood out-sources floats
Free of me of her of him of them a kind of subject-function
That divides and multiplies what I might become and then the plane levels
Thud on the padding swallowing hard I

Re-integrate my parts in the wrong order so I am a nightmare of a man
A nonhuman assemblage of human trash tasked with the inhuman demands
Of those fickle figures bent by gravity to the flat earth where veiny canals
Web the verdure or the smog of an industrial motorway valley gloats
Less real than the green light that twitches Lift Off (at last!)
That pushes me back in my seat torturers' bricks on my limbs
Drags me into heavy sky through the grip of bunching clouds
To darkness floating near-oblivion in non-place in non-time leaving me
Little relation to my accomplice American puffed up in his suit like a pastry
His fat thumbs-up veteran contempt for the European neophyte
Late arrival in the Space Age novice of Cold War heritage we rise
Flatten into floating orbit to confirm every mathematical calculation
Has been working towards the event we are the blending of machinic perceptions
A sentient metal exhalation that carries us safe a bubble of fresh air
To lock on the hulk of stale wheezing space station that in earth's breeze would be
Rusting like white goods on a tip but here is suspended pristine one
Measure of deceleration clear of throwing its hand down
Bored gambler falling in sparks from its orbit back to the allure
Of earth with its spaces that fill the senses and flood the mind with
Belonging where I don't belong off the page of my staging
All I can do is raise my visored head (against the pull of these terrestrial
Metaphors) and fix my eye upon the wobbling star that winks the squinty joke
Of dark matter advancing as if it were the light on the front of a train
Approaching our stop as if Gisele cries for the last time 'Are
We really a long way from Halle-Vilvoorde?' of that
Disputed illegitimate discounted place my home
I pull her closer to my chest that has breathed the air of no place
As though I could offer her some human consolation for the matter of space
For the matter of time's countdown estimated arrival alighting door-slam
We stand in the bilingual interval gifted by the arrivals display above
Or picked up as live GPS stream on Gisele's mobile throbbing
Against her shivering breast pensive with no thought or words our own
Torn from infinity we'd happily cleave our singularities
As the train berths at the platform's gusty docking-bay and we're
Wiped like a smudge of grease from a bar that is the last syllable of an ode
That croaks in the mouth of the doomed astronaut shrinking
In the very poem he intones ('my home')

His televised moment of terminal gasping metaphors
That float as universal humming antimatter's material epiphany
Swallowing hard not just miles but
Dimensions away from
(As a speck of my self boards the train back to)
Halle-Vilvoorde
Gisele


[1. Most Belgians retain a belief implanted in childhood that Tintin and Milou reached the moon by narrative means well before the Americans; see Hergé, *Destination Moon* and *Explorers on the Moon*. (Martin Krol)]

# Ode to Forme

*Be content with little; hope for nothing from the Great;*
*Moderate desire within justice's estate.*

from the Dutch and French of Christophe Plantin (1555-89):
Golden Compasses Officina Plantiniana Antwerp

**A** scholar hastens to the Sultan

       carries Ptolemaic geometry
(Latinised)
           ballistics for cannon
puffed pupa on a Turkish headland
       gifts from the Duke
            his rubricated vellum
      in ruby-encrusted bindings
his know-how his maps his incunabula
      printed and painted books bought from Plantin's shop


**O**n Cyprus Venetian

      customsmen
judge the scholar's mission
        intemperate and
turn him away folding
     a leaf down on the Byzantine apocryphon
         of West meeting East
       They pack him off to Brabant
back to his 'Munificent Master'
      sporting Polyglot apologies and Bible alike

# Ode to Zip

The pleasure boat turns under the bridge. It is spring twenty to three in the afternoon but not 1614. Every house wears a gable-face for the sky. Barges won't unload themselves. The men put their hands up the skirts of the light shades to check for current. The crowd blows its collective nose before boarding the tram. A drawbridge lifts and its only thanks is the smoke from the accelerating barge. Too big for the boat its funnel wheezes excuse. Cars cool on the deck of the ferry. Voice builds the chamber it fills syllable by syllable. Everybody walks nicely from the aeroplane it's been such a privilege to fly. Propellers hang motionless at Schipol waiting for that man's head there. Square buses amidst square cars leave the square buildings. It's not a smiling competition. Outside the café, the low backs of the girls' dresses allow the sun to kiss their necks. She topples from her bike but saves herself and her basket of groceries. Whipped dray horses trot the wet streets of Amsterdam. Fishing rods bend over the canal in an illusion of submarine opulence. The last rigging awaits the final sails and the ultimate departure. Ash from his fat cigar drops into the eels he's just gutted. The sensuous boy in the sailor suit strokes the model's rigging. They snog under the looming stern of the Atlantic liner. Twitching figures on the churning barrel-organ can't be said to be dancing. Tall buildings emblazoned with drying washing shimmer in their own canals. In Jordaan a trolley waits by the gutter as if it were about to discover its purpose. By the corner boys wrestle kick up their dusty heels. Before the royal palace peasants drop on the steps of the Dam. Dead protestant grandees are stirred by the military brass band eulogising three of god's creatures on the balcony. Human pyramids spontaneously built hoist one human to look at another. The blind accordionist ignores the clean pavement. Only the children are fooled that it really is Einstein or the Laughing Bishop. The black woman looks both ways admires the zebra crossing the coordination of the traffic lights' neat code but ignores the cankerous façade of the Post Office. Trams buses and bicycles throw the hieroglyph of the working week against this space of inhabitants and users. At least the broader canals offer room for the sky to blossom. Describe and aspire to do no more than describe the neat lawn that you think you will visit half a century hence to taste premium beer. Where there is water there are bikes leaning against railings and the people vanish. Snow on a boat moored at the canal-bank seems 'wrong'. Cars nosing up to the edge before the lurching buildings fill the dominated space which the imagination seeks to change. Dilation of space ingress and egress of mind is canaliculated. The crane framed below a bridge (with man on it gull above it) is less transformed than simply formed. Ex-form the boat its oar furred with snow. Through the room and through the next see flat against the wall Van Gogh's ear for music. The subject's on the dais his portrait's on the easel half formed. Hop onto your bike where the Nightwatchmen can't watch you as they draw back into their varnish. Rembrandt is a play of light on the wall while that man edges towards the other consumed with more than disinterest. Children litter the floor while the burghers pose. Appropriate the ex-forming snow daubing flower-heads beneath whatever it is you are meant to be gawping at in monumental wonder. Candles (unscented) hang amidst a geometry lesson from god. The lantern rests upon a table illuminating the chessboard floor though nothing moves. The zebra crossing forms zips across the colour field of the day to make us rescale. Chaotic scripts on music-stands give the game away. A swan advances beak aflame. The park steals the poet's name leaves him marooned among protestant angels. Square prams pushed by women in square dresses negotiate square patches of spring flowers. Three old men do not sit on the bench discussing what they did during the occupation. The elephant at the zoo does not discuss what it did during the occupation. The camels are like canals. Fifty years later you stop here and the boy kneeling on the cowl of his father's delivery bike is gone. At the corner of the bar two laughing girls grab the arms of the sailor who's trying to drink his beer. In the Blue Note he pulls the big laughing girl in bikini and gloves towards the dance floor. In Modernist physical space the Casino's punters sit between question mark alcoves make symbolic uses of its objects. After dark the hotel winks on the cooling bonnets of the cars. Under the netted ceiling absorbing the fug the masked women at the bar narrate the space they live through from their bodies that live through it. They dance as the crooner lifts his eyes to heaven and serenades miscegenation. She necks her wine black gloves somehow giving her away before she's taken. The sixteen year old leans back knowing it will push her breasts out but doesn't see the plump hand thrusting a huge cigarette packet into her back. Swings swing where the corpses once swung before the Waag. Amid the spangled gynecopia of chorus girl slutdom she sucks a bottle of Coke and rests her tired twinkle-toes. The man in the dress surrounded by be-plumed women is the only one to carry flowers he must be special. Time is curled in a hollow without shadow without echo without rhyme. Later it's Amsterdam 1959 again and lit buildings smudge the canals with their de-formations. The Westertoren narrows in stages towards the night. In morning light staggered houses totter towards the sun. The Sally Army marches down Zeedjik to distract us from the Heineken sign on the Chinese. Later graduands knock on basement windows to ask for chips and mayonnaise. She exfoliates from her door ex-formed opening its promise as chair and light-shade mimic domesticity and murmurs invitations to something unspoken. Gossip from high windows spits onto cobbles. He's frozen feet in slush hands melting in hot pockets. Rags heaped on the ground where the dog sniffs could remind these people of Belsen but they turn away their square backs tucked under rectangular awnings. The Indonesian housewife is happy with limp leeks wrapped in Dutch. A glass of grey milk rests on the edge while she scrapes Nazis' fingers from the inside of a leather glove. Describe and aspire to do more than describe these distrustful eyes staring at you over cauliflowers. More corpses of clothes at Waterlooplein. Beards hang over books on the stall that Spinoza that van der Vondel that ode diligently unfinished. Trail a finger along the sides of dusty vitrines in the Museum of Amnesia. By the cages they discuss dinosaur-beetles bull-head gulls ferret-fish. Bananas fight like tuna to leap into the vendor's till. The Torah expounded he looks up at the women in the grilled gallery and doesn't allow his next thought to form. Fifty years later he's still polishing the same diamond. Withered flowers at the feet of the heroes turn to garbage. A lump of lard compacted on a plinth bellows at the clouds that grizzle away. The order of the city from the air is a jumble you arrive to dis-en-form. A chorus of chimneys sings energy to the skies. The basket-ball boys are stunned by the ball that hangs for three seconds over its basket. His hat flies off over the crowd and swoops under the goalpost startling the goalie not trained beyond the rules of the game. Rhyme drops from line-endings like blossom like a forgetting of memory like likeness itself. The mosaic can be re-formed to form any image you want. Square glass on the square building reflects the day and we will all loyally work in it for a hundred years. A heavy pile is driven into the ground to attempt to hold this city together for one more day.

# Twitterodes

for my followers and for the
followers of my followers

▪ 100 (twittersonnet)

bearded ev
ergreen ov
erflowing
a craggy c

astle wall
/bag of ce
ment flat
ened and b

roken on t
ramlines t
o leave du

st/bike bu
ckled wher
e it hangs

▪ 99 piggybacking girls round the monument/NEPTUNE stamping his horses (a café steals his water thunder)/black tooth windows/ladies sipping ORVAL ▪ 98 a moorhen and fluffed chick stand on the girder wet webs safe from tidal flow/all motion is relative/cannot be seen beyond their conception ▪ 97 Time dies. Oak leaves spread at water-level. As many roofs on display as at a roofers' convention. How many maps to deal with a given space? ▪ 96 time at the heart of space is movement/the rear of the fish restaurant lurching into the river/the empty boat with outboard bobbing/creaking ▪ 95 the buttressed bulge below defeated windows/cannot be seen beyond their conception hoisted from river/sagging over the waterline on the bend ▪ 94 the buttressed bulge below defeated windows/analysis destroyed the solidity of this fisherman's house/sagging over the waterline on the bend ▪ 93 she's reading a book to remind her how a saint should act or:/a critique of space high above the Botermarkt/halo or crown/a forlorn corner ▪ 92 chancels with bats' wings architecture out of Hell creating the illusion of time/cars parked like odd shoes lined up under a hat-stand/blent ▪ 91 green ironwork crawls up the side of the building/mental and social at once/over the way where I park my bike/Ghent where I have never lived ▪ 90 his arm with hands in pockets of gesture among parcels of space/mustard gas forest seeps across paths of ice/his lowered head a wan pellicle ▪ 89 faces constructed by background (interference)/bodies shudder into ice-floe paint-flick a texture of rainbow lemon and tree blot/in creases ▪ 88 stroll through a world of scratches slashing burning grounded by the medium without message sinking into its impositions/fingerflicking ▪ 87 past her snarl windows across the canal she tightens her open cup leotard adjusts crotchless crotch lets the world pass brushing her breasts ▪ 86 something fishy about the body/head grafted from myth/curved to the tree that sways behind its back/no arms or branches but toes and roots ▪ 85 the bushes look like huddled hedgehogs with their backs turned/how many maps might be needed to deal with this given space to code or decode ▪ 84 the code is more deceptive than the thing when the thing is an acorn on a column or an empty plaque embossed with graffiti ▪ 83 thru' marble arch tarpaulin on which Magritte's curtain-building is opening on flat summer skies (behind which dreams the renovating palace) ▪ 82 cloven hooves aloft double breath spout/a floating medium latticed with lacy rippled contrast/class war ▪ 81 the subject cannot do without the object pleading in the language of things: of handsized bricks/cut glass/cones conjured from flat tiles ▪ 80 objects swamped by facts or/spitting into a little cup/ejaculations/measured by money/wishing well full of best wishes/vacant inscriptions ▪ 79 patiently sit all day arms folded head bent into space complete with vanishing point spewing a lip-moulded stream of eternal spittle ▪ 78 sliced buildings profess professions/professors abstract perspective inscribing human relations across the square/crowds gawp/clouds glower ▪ 77 ODE TO DIVERSITY/ gilded trinkets tumbling down the face of the Museum of Amnesia/Hindu woman miming destitution with anguished fists: kerbed ▪ 76 laboured place/floral bolts into wood/a dragon sheered through/hand raised (swordless)/shield shielding nothing/ruthless eyes & hacked nose ▪ 75 inside the frame resembles everything else/repetitious spaces repeated within repeating scenes of the Markt selling itself to itself/outside ▪ 74 rows of lights under gables compose the square/a statue does not know that it is one/issuing orders or delivering blessings/texture blooms ▪ 73 a set of real operations made the man in a kagoul bend over to examine the dog's arse/ another set made the dog-cobbles-bollards-street-city ▪ 72 stone dog cocking a leg against the corner bollard rue des Chartreux monumentalising the quotidian moment fleeting active yet still on guard ▪ 71 each pinnacle pinched with gestures/hands spread, legs tossed, torsos twisted, heads bent/no faces under hats to challenge a scythe of cloud ▪ 70 'Il faut être absolument moderne'/ICI OÙ PAUL VERLAINE BLESSA ARTHUR RIMBAUD D'UN COUP DE REVOLVER ▪ 69 story twists as the narrator turns (blue pen marks on his thigh/some eye sorts this out/foliage entwines marble) turns to caress the hidden ▪ 68 he appeared from the skies (an hour or so ago) skin scaly oily carbuncular and craterous unshaven/pores collecting the grit of this world ▪ 67 leaf tickles founder's ear/hand around shoulder/above finny cloak that superhumanises/bleached face adorned with felt-tip moustaches/and me ▪ 66 projective space for projectile voicings projected onto you as responsibility's double breath ▪ 65 put this back on the map: (t)race the webbed salute/the contorted leap (fixed)/the water breath against a rhythm of cars-trees-lampposts ▪ 64 punch up on a pinpoint squalid flailing in a narrative that covers its tracks like a map of porous borders on the point of being torn into ▪ 63 which map's he on/giving his game away escapes the arcade with jacket over shoulder scowling/invisibility unplotted/a post-it in a phone box ▪ 62 as quick as mind he sleeps in a chair curved like a wave carrying his outdoor dreams hands folded liver spotted the city map ▪ 61 un soldat inconnu competing with discourses to travel to a ring of growling gryphons holding up the dish of flame for een onbekende soldaat ▪ 60 aloft column beyond gilded fringe Léopold heading up clouds/ below gold extracted from the (c)ore of the 1831 constitution ▪ 59 Function as ornament. A choice of walls packages the day. You could talk excrescence into style. Figures twisted into narrative stall. ▪ 58 figures twisted into narrative move as soon as you near bleed from eye sockets rumble into your body space (Johan Muyle) ▪ 57 this writing is not a body/stumps along beside rails (cracked dish carries its flame) steps on grass scratches head/ this body isn't writing ▪ 56 'because the world is in colour' (explains Abbas): the black and white bride marries the corpse in the photo they hold next to her ▪ 55 salmon brick house on the rise beyond the canal too low to register upon whatever it is that records windows punctured with Flemish darkness ▪ 54 a pagan flap of wings and tangle of talons over a body frozen and erected to the status of myth/beyond the wire cupped tulips multiple arch ▪ 53 macro glass in its flat and curved space varieties abutted/micro figurative dummy catching the taint of the city on its greening skin ▪ 52 the day is occurring to itself we walk into it and I think with the back of my head facing it • 51 I'm the man under the hedge arch looking at the dome of Le Botanique/you are the one who sees me beyond the lily pond framed by your looking • 50 I'm a lamppost man a lawn corpse man a pigeon man a straight path man a modernist man a hedge twig man a UFO flash in the dark trees man • 49 pulsions of perfect embodiedness the roof steps into cloud masturbating a place in blacked-out childhood forever under construction • 48 inscribed in me: me at the attic window the space of me looking out over Lievestraat and the cellar window peeping at passers' ankles knees • 47 glass buildings in non-utile shapes refract each other narrowing sky spoutspray steaming below/hoisted man washes his way around the curves • 46 BETWEEN sagging leaves and crouching fur/soft feet and hard cobbles/canopied shade and light so naked it is invisible/ WEAVES TIME'S QUESTION • 45 horsechestnuthands wave over water/ internationalbrickwork leads to the fountain/waterspouthalo behind the vigilstatue/THINK: where are we • 44 column sprouting/horns of a devil// or family tree as gurgling/gargoyles//the impression of feet/on the cobbles prints unreadable/history • 43 rotate to landscape: shadowed archway a reservoir of ink or/pitch sky with horizon of bricklight/crabplants scuttling wherever's up • 42 heraldic ensigns horizonless on the thick glass of the windows of the Huys der Liefde/pulled inside out a house of Lipsius/ Montanus/Ortelius • 41 unseatable throne? • 40 rhinolalia muzzle nudges for a broken song • 39 aloft surveying all that isn't his mistaken for shirtless carving beside stirring gauze that screens the equine statue/its doubtful gestures • 38 reclusive Balthasar's golden compass grips the globe crippled inky fingers measure the surface of maps the ridges of print on finest paper • 37 the marvellous is awkward/scribbling among Plantin's shelves dialoguing with categories the moment's historian shot through with knowledge • 36 produce this house as you move through it reading the print and map rooms navigating your history thinking about what's not present/leaning • 35 Plantin's image rises from brickwork latticed windows like uncut sheets: proofread the bookish house looking inward to its garden • 34 of the material where material is stone as solid as stone should be between praxis and representation: lion propped up on its human fist • 33 moss on the bark of the tree like green light it may go around the world we live it and we think it and it thinks us in its living • 32 scowling Christ with sword and scales the twisted Host a print of the Spanish Fury identities fixed throwntogetherness without scatter • 31 letters reversed on milky window absent depth unmarked by time and drainpipes spewing tendrillar wires that sing Latvia Estonia Finland • 30 frame the red window frame which frames the curved cream underbelly of the stairs and the varnished wood banisters which follow them ▪ 29 spatial scales stepped roofs encounter flows of flags abstractions of maps tides of information against waves of nostalgia catching light ▪ 28 space outwith place where roofs meet sky: on false chimneys or high points: gold eagle/alert fox/be-piked yeoman/mariner shading his eyes ▪ 27 silver crown midpoint over iron gateway a compression point funnelling people: space-time coordinate for inter-species solidarity ▪ 26 the segmented reflection of the outer window ghosted its ornate patterns of authority its relative position beyond glass in focal illusion ▪ 25 a priori steps of Antwerp station where people produce (carrying pushchairs lifting children hauling rucksacks) pause by marble pillars/noon ▪ 24 flat planes of faces curve as intervals in negative distance a single red flag flutters on a window ledge white motif curled shyly away ▪ 23 three men in sou'westers tend towards the Swiss poster promising 'More than meets the eye' in English/bent one way-street sign arrowing ▪ 22 lateral shots of words past floral baskets gilded cornices irregularly stepped balconies café parasols the logos of international exchange ▪ 21 guild houses round the Markt surface cut to the depths of the manifesto: shoulder to shoulder their tight asperities ▪ 20 sculpted sleep as lids are moulded shut/a masturbator's grip upon the mayoral scroll LEONARD VANDENHECKE ▪ 19 tensions in space not forms cut into (our) time they are floating not waiting striking out not enduring ▪ 18 the closer you get the less there is (approach as an eye) abrupt delineations that are read as shaded building bricks on a 2D matrix ▪ 17 crouch under the ledge upon which the knight stretches an overstepping toe the space and scope left for the roughed in/beyond genealogy ▪ 16 rows of knives scissors for variation a syntax of blades behind the window of the coutellerie a razor's discrimination between flesh and air ▪ 15 synchronic pan: Flemish with crane aloft/an ice façade drips/to fore: fountain where Calder mobile swings like a sail but dances in time ▪ 14 decompartment-alisation of externals: glass for clouds and girders blossoming style on the superface/for depth: old perfume old iron ▪ 13 fixed point or vortex/canopied ingress egress/the solidity of glass held by black wrought ironwork a cage for shoppers musical instruments ▪ 12 tactical formations of repetition: conical trees amid scratched bark plane/hedges and gangly stems/garbage urns/pools of dust turds in sand ▪ 11 brickwork syntax with wide cement connectives hanging there and/or sculpted there heraldic and abstracted the shell of the shell ▪ 10 more an homunculus bent knees whorish pelvic stretch: the curved water pipe up his arse launches a parabola his eternal stream completes ▪ 9 not botticellian scalloped arrival dispersal of piss-steam piddle-trickle the smallest statue of illiberality in the world ▪ 8 blue wall pixellated in close-up winged with cracking paintwork steps down which mythic characters chase in contiguity/coincidence/overload ▪ 7 nose into perspective (skip with a rope on the roof) smell basket of flowers red and purple synthesised into the spaces you sniff out ▪ 6 a slash across a speckled sky/the slope of the roof/the tilt of an eye//time full of now perspective ▪ 5 not the heavy timbers of the shadowy door but the saints poised for studied martyrdom in slanted sunlight tinting ingress ▪ 4 De Grote Markt/carve supernal genealogies onto each spatial container/or: float them there as if by human intention ▪ 3 Doric Bourse time makes KNACK space in place of crossing experience with body lurching motorbike at rest against wall of bleached exchange ▪ 2 spire at dusk spearing vapour trails a lone gull gliding above the pinnacle of Europe flecked wash over clenched dark buildings ▪1 breathing water spout against an irradiated dusk ripple ▪ 0 tweets @ www.twitter.com/ Van Valckenborch 2009-2008

## *from* EUOIA: 27 Translations

(EUOIA: European Union of Imaginary Authors website/e-books for Kindle, etc.
/pdf downloads/poetics statements and supposed interviews @ www.euoia.be)


Jurgita Zujūtė (1966- ) Lithuania


## *Kybartai Noctune*

what is that sound
humming like an antique fridge packed with ice

the hint of a turbine something turning
a patient siren rising and falling

perhaps it's merely the sound of maintenance men
on the railway hi-viz jackets between last train and first
testing the line

it's a tumour on the flanks of night
this voice its pain rising and falling
a suspiration perhaps within me
the benign whine of my nervous system

but it's more like negative space
growling in shadows beside the glowing curtain
sound-motes floating in the eye of my audition

darkness breathing pure light or
the broken reed of a pigeon's throat gasping toward dawn

Lucia Ciancaglini (1968-2010) Italy

## from &

& I rest all morning nestling my lava java
        an empty sleeve salutes the cosh of exclamation
& cogs within cognition spit forth these forms

& an ampersand ghosted on the wall over from the coffee shop
        is a hollow in a headlock with nothing to say to us
& there's too much for the mind to do each second

& my son crayons the zero round & round & round &
        knuckling gloves on my lip gloss tease my melting eyes
& patterned interferences wipe the bootprint off my smile

& framed by sculpted hair I wait for the sky to drop
        to flood my bleached floss with grey light
& a lash of uncoiling ampersand cracks in the slanted hail

(Cork, 2010)

Jitka Průchová (1978-) Czech Republic

## Herat 1978

*after the photographs of Bohumil Krčil*

Town walls of dust ring men of dust
Walking in dusty air to buy and sell dust

(Bread was stone once laid on stone tables
The hollow reservoir now brick and brick dust)

A live tree flourishes like a dead bush
Timber forests the mind in leafless plenitude

A dog guards the kiln its ceramic kennel
The upper windows higher than a camel's hump

*You wait until the Russians get here*
*We'll grind them into dust and populate the winds!*

## Trine Kragelund (1979-) Denmark

### *Nonofesto*

no poetics
no ideas
no power
no 'poems'
no edits
no fidelity
no interruption
no nouns
no prosody
no flesh
no form
no genre
no things
no typing
no psychology
no representation
no symptomology
no disjunction
no motivation
no plumbing
no interferences
no affect
no noems
no transgression
no philosophy
no technique
no subversion
no empathy
no delight
no vanguard
no enjambment
no conceptualism
no fiction

no ecstasy
no no
no gender
no goats
no poet
no sonnets
no 'we'
no message
no conjunction
no noise
no shining
no record
no silence
no jumps
no entropy
no map

## Sophie Poppmeier (1981-) Austria

### Book 1 Poem 1

All propositions in poems
are fictions I know
except in this one, otherwise
why would I write it now?

It sits where I sit enlanguaging
what it enlanguages at the centre
of 'my fabulous continent'
which, like the middle of an

old record overplayed clumsily,
is a loose black hole that's
unfit for purpose, whose purpose was
to repeat what's already been performed.

I lie in wait for the new lyric
which lies low, lying like hell
in heavenly form. It echoes
my chants to change my life.

(2000)

# Rue des Chartreaux
# The Diary of Annemie Dupuis

Monday 19 July 2010

I've searched for Van Valckenborch for months, for years even, first with Martin, then on my own. The question *where are you?* abbreviates as *are you?*

How does one determine that one has successfully found nothing? Nothing turns up with a vengeance. I line success with disquiet.

You left too many clues that you didn't exist for me not to believe that you did.

Do.

Your rhythm of appearance—each new poem—syncopated with the rhythm of your non-appearances, missed dates nagging on Martin's iPhone.

'Objects, landscapes, events, people, give me much pleasure. I am composed of their variety, which would allow me to exist even in silence,' you quoted Ponge, almost shouting on your page. But it wasn't enough.

Poetic *voice*: is this not proof of linguistic and philosophic sclerosis?

Your cognitive prosody: the pleasure of speed against *la petite mort* of each line break.

Line by line this diary is structuring me for you.


Saturday 24 July 2010

Time to manage my online profile, as Martin would say. Deleted Facebook, deleted Twitter. A blank screen, the cursor winking with me.

Threw away Martin's last clothes, the odd book.

Cancelled appointments with hairdresser, translation agency, doctor.

Gathered your poems and arranged them as if in surrender to an archive, appropriate to their *inachevée*. Slammed the file shut like a cell door.

Escaped as far as the canal to watch rain pelting hypnotic beats upon the tarpaulin of a barge swaying at its moorings. Stood on the Porte de Flandre for an hour. The sole of my broken shoe sponging up Brussels.


Sunday 25 July 2010

I'd always seen the formal empathy of my translations as naked masks, voice masks, *après tu*. Martin believed that one was making 'versions' and had the licence, obligation, to tamper. But Martin had a different task, working with your aprosody, your 'principle of interruption', your spatial poetics.

No poet had—has—written equally in Flemish and Walloon since Liliane Wouters. 'We are all Franskiljons, we poets,' wrote Hugo Claus.

A sheet of rain mutes the chimes of distant church bells. Competing *chanteurs*.


Tuesday 27 July 2010

Emails from Canderlinck about poems in German, supposed to be by you, so obviously fake I don't reply. Everybody's getting in on the act. I delete my email account.

In the café by the church I plunge my ringing phone into a glass of Rodenbach. Acids bite at the lines of communication to the doctor. The barman throws up his arms, my last chance. I'm out.

Customers envelop themselves in *De Morgen* or *Le Soir*. Six weeks without a government.

The song of the phone curdles in its own throat.

A fine drizzle in warm air falls like love should. By the gurgling pissoir. Its 'metrical intelligence', as you would say.

In rue de Flandre, where I flee to the little bar with leather diamonds on the wall and seats you could slide off, I listen to guttural Flemish spoken by men who look like they're from Rodenbach adverts. Grizzled and begrimed. Framed in black and white, contrast set to max. Their smoke-lined voices funnelling phlegm. Like you?


Wednesday 28 July 2010

I've just travelled the length of rue Antoine Dansaert to search for vegetables, still can't catch Brussels demotic with my Canadian-Parisian French. In certain moods I do feel I've invented you, stamped you with English. I build you up from figures in the street: existential translation, mad flânerie. Under the arcade a man about thirty-five squeezes cauliflowers with too much zeal. His narrow shades, slightly hunched shoulders, suggest some collectables. He smiles, sly. I add his details to the identikit. A translated man.

'Have you never thought that my body would disintegrate if ever it entered the twisted stuff of words?' a creature of Nicole Brossard has it.

You're nearly finished. One more sweep around Bozar on a wet Thursday afternoon and you'll be complete.

Sunday 1 August 2010

A dream. You were in court, going down for spying for Holland or Luxembourg or Latvia. As you were led away you waved to Martin. Who was it that said all poets are spies? Writing coded messages (about us), keeping secrets (from us).

Like the Welsh girl upstairs. Let's call her Bethany.

I taught her French and we became lovers.

She wanted to brush up her Dutch so Martin taught her too. One Wednesday they ran away together.

Let's keep this story neat.

Early spring light fading too low to read any more, we elide on her narrow bed—she whimpers, whispers in Welsh.

*Their* trashing sex after the jazz club, one cocktail too many: the ceiling shudders, the light shimmers.

To unlove, to dislove. To unexist, to re-exist, to re-un-exist? Is this possible, if I can first make them exist in some imagined movement of their love-making?

Or you, whose benign absence I construct from solid shadow?


Tuesday 3 August 2010

I start every day on a naked encounter with your roll and tumbling tercets. I see the problem for the first time, at the very moment that it is solved, as you appear in the corporeality of expression. A patch of unpolished silver shifting in grey cloud burns my eyes. I'm writing you up, an experiment conducted upon my body. Metrics as breakage, as you said. I have begun to feel the muscle of your last poem flexing close on my wet cheek, dry lips. Cow.


Wednesday 4 August 2010

Tuesday I finished you. A wet morning deciding on a moustache or not. Not.

If I were to pull off your clothes, hold you in my arms, make to scratch your back in my ecstasy, I would claw my own breast. Caesurae in air.

Rain in Place Ste-Catherine all afternoon. Speckling the surface of the fountains, washing the slabs of cigarette butts, driving them along mossy runnels. Your vectoral poetics.

Into the apartment above has moved a Catalan, Cristòfol Subira. The mouse squeak of a floorboard. He's a poet. Believe it. Or not.

Saturday 7 August 2010

A chaos of papers, a punnet of North Sea food, a bottle of cheap red on my writing desk by the window. Uninterrupted scratches of rain.

Now I've put you together and you won't work, the others are falling apart. I see them in pieces: Bethany uncoiled from a silk gown, a slither of weepy meat. Martin as unfurled foreskin after a bath, glans speckled and swelling.

During the night, crapulent and shaky, I went down to the concierge, his damp cubby-hole by the main door, lit only by his television. It flickered the news: nine weeks without a government.

'Nobody here of that name,' he said, as I asked. 'Just Hubert Zuba, that poetry guy from Malta. I've seen him on the box.'

What did I expect? John Shade, Ricardo Reis, Bob McCorkle, Luis Antonio Sensini? Sturla Jón Jónsson?

He looked at me oddly, stubbed his cigarette out, and turned as though to speak at length.

I noticed that my apartment on the wall-chart he'd peered at was marked VACANT.

Sunday 8 August 2010

If I were to walk out of this apartment, cross the road by L'Archiduc, risk the lurching cars and angry klaxons, and be run over—the last of the tablets have gone—you would continue, consistent, though I would not know this. Wouldn't you?

If I were to walk out of the apartment, bags sent on in advance, and head for the Metro, to leave this phantasmal location at last, you would begin to exist in the only way you could make sense. I might see you everywhere, nodding, familiar, on the Metro, hanging onto a rocking leather strap like a mountaineer, or waving with delight through the mute security glass between arrivals and departures at the airport. It wouldn't matter.

If Martin is with Bethany or without her (bless her little Celtic nipples!) he sits on his flight back to Durban. Perhaps. In his briefcase a photocopy of your last Flemish poem, peppered with annotations and ready for a serious airborne session.

If I settle into my famous seat over the wing, preparing my ears for the pressure of take-off—two stops to Quebec—what is the chance you might rustle into the seat next to me and say, 'Hey, that's no way to say goodbye'?


Thursday 12 August 2010

I'm sitting in the dock, moist hand clinging to grimy rail. The courtroom of some Eastern European capital. Standing beside myself I know this is a dream.

I'm accused of people-trafficking, but I don't know why.

Questioned through an interpreter, it strikes me. I have made up a fictional national poet—his name at least—by combining the forename and surname with the most diacritics in the language, the least vowels. But it's also the name of a villain. The unshaven giant with the scar down his face whispering curses to a solicitor in a bursting shiny suit. The police must have found my notes, tangles of names.

I realise the improbability of my alibi, the impossibility of communicating this. The interpreter squints at me, lost.

I hear my name mispronounced by the judge in his frayed crimson gown. I am nudged to my feet. He looks through me.

Sophie Poppmeier of Austria, Erik Canderlinck of Belgium (Wallonia), Paul Coppens of Belgium (Flanders), Gurkan Arnavut of Cyprus, Jitka Průchová of the Czech Republic, Lucia Ciancaglini of Italy, Jurgita Zujūtė of Lithuania, Hubert Zuba of Malta, Maarten De Zoete of Holland, Trine Kragelund of Denmark, Cristòfol Subira of Spain (Catalunya). Yes, yes, stop there, at that one.

I wake in a spray of sweat.


Friday 13 August 2010

I laugh in a spray of sweat, swallowed by pillows, buoyed by the churned mattress.

Post-coital, soft and confessional, Cristòfol murmurs that he writes poems in Spanish as well as Catalan. Quite different ones, as it happens. I take a quick shower. I must avoid this again, affect indifference, even cruelty. I return rubbing my hair. When he presses into me, I bite his tongue. There's blood.

It works.

Within hours I'm moved out. The stone dog on the corner of rue des Chartreux cocks its leg higher as I dip into the dark interior of a white car. Ah! Rue des Chartreaux, where Verlaine loaded the fateful pistol.

It's unlikely that you'd let me go like this. Properly speaking, I do not exist, which shouldn't stop me generating effects.

You are my special effect.

You sit at a café table, outside in the square at Antwerp, laptop open, eyes aloft. You spot a roofer surveying the city, easily mistaken for a carving he's so still, beside stirring gauze that screens a half-restored statue. You feed this perception into a Twitterode for your following—juggling letters, spaces, words—and go offline with a satisfied click. Your coffee arrives, steam coiling into air. Too early for De Koninck. Your day has yet to warm.

Then you write me up, in an encrypted file, where the writer really lives, deep in his hard-drive.

And set me free.

In it you will then write what you want. No-one will read it, no-one will translate it, but no-one will doubt that it's real. No-one will even harbour the ghost of a suspicion that you exist.

Start from there René Van Valckenborch.

# Acknowledgements

I owe the title of this volume to Marina Warner's description of Edward Said.

Thanks to Nicholas Royle (*Antwerp*) for inspiration and Zoë Skoulding for bringing Gurkan Arnavut to life with me.

Some of these poems appear in the following publications: *Adirondack Review, AND, Damn the Ceasars! Ekleksographia, Form & Fontanelles, Holdfire Press blog* (holdfirepress.wordpress.com), *Poetry Salzburg, Poetry Wales, Roundyhouse, Sugar Mule, Sunfish, Tears in the Fence, The Other Room Anthology 5, VLAK, The Wolf.*

Some appear on *The Claudius App*, as text at theclaudiusapp.com/3-sheppard.html and as audio file at theclaudiusapp.com/3-amp.html.

Some appear as poetry prints made with Pete Clarke at poetrybeyondtext. org/clarke-sheppard.html for the AHRC project *Poetry Beyond Text.*

The 100 'Twitterodes' appear on Twitter at twitter.com/#!/VanValckenborch. and are collected on *Pages* at robertsheppard.blogspot.com, 31 December 2010. Some additionally appear with photographs on *Pages* between 26 November and 30 December 2010.

A performance of part of 'background pleasures' may be viewed at vimeo. com/13739658

Van Valckenborch's 'uncollected prose', 'Frozen Cuts of Light: The Scratch Cinema of Paul Coppens' may be read on Lyndon Davies' *Junction Box* at lyndondavies.co.uk/w/655/robert-sheppard-frozen-cuts-of-light-the-scratch-cinema-of-paul-coppens/

There is a Van Valckenborch page on my website at robertsheppard.weebly. com/rene-van-valckenborch.html.

Thanks to all the dedicated editors and activists who first published these works.

Lightning Source UK Ltd.
Milton Keynes UK
UKOW040604200613

212545UK00001B/27/P